50
RELATIVES
WORSE
THAN
YOURS

50
RELATIVES
WORSE
THAN
YOURS

Justin Racz

with Alec Brownstein

BLOOMSBURY

Published by Bloomsbury Publishing, New York and London
Distributed to the trade by Holtzbrinck Publishers

All papers used by Bloomsbury Publishing are natural, recyclable products made from
wood grown in well-managed forests. The manufacturing processes conform to the environ-
mental regulations of the country of origin.

Library of Congress Cataloging-in-Publication Data has been applied for.

ISBN 1-59691-055-0
ISBN-13 978-1-59691-055-3

First U.S. Edition 2005

1 3 5 7 9 10 8 6 4 2

Designed by Justin Racz and Elizabeth Van Itallie
Printed and bound in Singapore by Tien Wah Press Ltd

For our families. Please forgive us.

_____

"All happy families are alike;
each unhappy family is unhappy in its own way."
—Leo Tolstoy, *Anna Karenina*

Relatives

1. The Perfect Family
2. Back on the Singles Scene Dad
3. Child Who Was in a National TV Commercial
4. Really Firm Handshaker
5. Grandpa Speedo
6. Happy Ex-Wife
7. Inga, Swedish Au Pair
8. Buffet Loiterers
9. Holistic New Age Aunt
10. Raging Alcoholic Masquerading as a Wine Connoisseur
11. NASCAR Family
12. The Child Substitute
13. Girl Scout Troop Leader Mom
14. Gold Digger (a.k.a. Pumpkin)
15. Uncle Stan the Camera Man
16. Slightly Racist Grandparent
17. Fanny, Not the Life of the Party
18. Your Son, the Tenant
19. *America's Most Wanted* Cousin
20. Conversation Hijacker
21. Power-Hungry Hosts
22. Sister Who Was in *Girls Gone Wild*
23. Jewish Mother
24. Family Newsletter Publisher

1. The Perfect Family

PROFILE

Dad's a lawyer with his own practice. Mom's an art therapist at the children's hospital. Little Becky is on the ice hockey Olympics Development team; Little Bobby is on the state chess team. Basically, imagine everything good about your family, double it, and subtract all that's bad. That's them.

GIFT

A monogrammed L.L. Bean tote bag—therefore, you can't return it.

MOTTO

"You can do anything in life if you put your mind to it. *And* have a good lawyer!"

HOME

The opposite of your home.

BENEFITS

You have the same last name. Makes you look better when trying to get your kids into the same school.

DRAWBACKS

Spending time with them makes you want to go on Prozac.

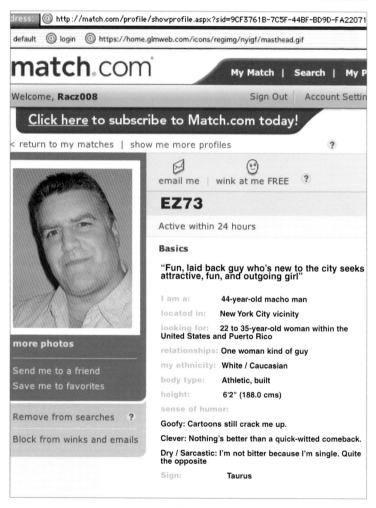

dress: @ http://match.com/profile/showprofile.aspx?sid=9CF3761B-7C5F-44BF-BD9D-FA22071

default @ login @ https://home.glmweb.com/icons/regimg/nyigf/masthead.gif

match.com

My Match | Search | My P

Welcome, **Racz008**

Sign Out | Account Settin

<u>Click here</u> to subscribe to Match.com today!

< return to my matches | show me more profiles ?

email me | wink at me FREE ?

EZ73

Active within 24 hours

Basics

"Fun, laid back guy who's new to the city seeks
attractive, fun, and outgoing girl"

I am a:	**44-year-old macho man**
located in:	**New York City vicinity**
looking for:	**22 to 35-year-old woman within the United States and Puerto Rico**
relationships:	**One woman kind of guy**
my ethnicity:	**White / Caucasian**
body type:	**Athletic, built**
height:	**6'2" (188.0 cms)**

sense of humor:

Goofy: Cartoons still crack me up.

Clever: Nothing's better than a quick-witted comeback.

Dry / Sarcastic: I'm not bitter because I'm single. Quite
the opposite

Sign:	**Taurus**

more photos

Send me to a friend

Save me to favorites

Remove from searches ?

Block from winks and emails

2. Back-on-the-Singles-Scene Dad

PROFILE

He's making up for lost time by Internet dating—sites like Match.com, eHarmony, JDate, Nerve.com, AmericanSingles.com. According to his profile, he likes water sports, the *New York Times* crossword puzzle, and travel.

GIFT

He's spent enough on the kids and the wife. Now it's his turn—hello, Mazda Miata.

MOTTO

"I'm new to this, but I thought I'd give it a shot."

HOME

Rents a furnished condo across town. On the weekends you can go swimming at the building's *Melrose Place*–like pool.

BENEFITS

He's now a lot cooler about curfew and TV time.

DRAWBACKS

Running into him at a club.

3. Child Who Was in a National TV Commercial

He's really cute—until he starts reciting his audition monologues.

He autographs the holiday card and sends you boxes of free cake mix.

"Mmm, mmm choctastic!"

He has more money than you do. It's now in a money market fund compounding interest.

A child actor's career has a very short lifespan.

He just bought his parents their dream house on Lake Arrowhead. Beats the pinecone bird feeder you made for your mom when you were nine.

4. Really Firm Handshaker

PROFILE

At family parties, you avoid him like the plague to keep your fingers from being crushed in his viselike grip.

GIFT

A free lesson in Street Fighting 101. Classes taught between holiday meals include the quarter nelson, the kidney punch, and the knee to the groin.

MOTTO

"Put 'er there! What? You call that a handshake?"

FAME

Was an extra in the arm-wrestling film *Over the Top,* starring Academy Award winner Sylvester Stallone.

BENEFITS

In an effort to be hip, he has started to transition to the high five.

DRAWBACKS

Will break a rib if he bear-hugs you.

5. Grandpa Speedo

PROFILE

No one is sure when he started the tradition of wearing a frighteningly tight loincloth on family vacations. But it won't stop.

GIFT

One-month membership at Hollywood Tan.

MOTTO

"Another nice day to relax in a banana hammock."

SECRET

Doesn't know how to swim.

BENEFITS

Guaranteed to empty the most crowded hotel swimming pool.

DRAWBACKS

Needs help getting suntan lotion on those hard-to-reach places.

6. Happy Ex-Wife

PROFILE

Now that she's your ex, she's never been happier. In fact, she just threw herself a divorce party and invited all your friends.

GIFT

Viagra.

MOTTO

"Everyone throw their keys into the bowl!"

SECRET

Serves you right, you made out with the intern at the company Christmas party.

BENEFITS

At least you got the convertible in the settlement.

DRAWBACKS

Your ex-best friend is now dating your ex-wife, playing with your ex-dog, and spending the night in your ex-bed.

7. Inga, Swedish Au Pair

PROFILE

To the teenage son, she's the stepsister he never had but always wanted. For Dad, the perfect cure for the seven-year itch. For Mom, free child care in exchange for lodging.

GIFT

She's neat, she loves the children, she doesn't mind chores, she's hot—a gift for the entire family.

MOTTO

"Rormiginte!"
("Don't touch me!")

SECRET

She doesn't love ABBA.

BENEFITS

For Junior, it could be the sexual awakening that *Penthouse Forums* are made of.

DRAWBACKS

Her visa expires next year.

8. Buffet Loiterers

PROFILE

They treat family functions like an All-U-Can-Eat Buffet. They traveled over 300 miles and are darn sure gonna get enough chicken fingers, bagels and lox, and strawberry tarts to compensate for it.

GIFT

Don't expect anything this year. Gas prices are through the roof.

MOTTO

"Nicholas, eat more smoked salmon—don't waste your time on pasta."

HOME

No idea. It's never been seen.

BENEFITS

There was nothing good at Great-Uncle Phil's funeral so they went out and grabbed a bucket of KFC.

DRAWBACKS

Kiss the shrimp cocktail goodbye.

9. Holistic New Age Aunt

PROFILE

Shops at Whole Foods, doesn't wear fur, listens to Enya and believes we should only eat what we grow or slaughter with our own hands.

GIFT

Dreamcatcher, healing crystal, oracle cards, aromatherapy, hydrotherapy, Jamba Juice gift certificate.

WARDROBE

Loose, formless linen or hemp pants; large beaded ethnic jewelry; rainbow shawl for all seasons.

FAME

Channeled the spirit of dead Grandpa Jack at Thanksgiving six years ago.

BENEFITS

Can score you some killer pot.

DRAWBACKS

Knows someone in the same Kabbalah class as Madonna but refuses to introduce you because that would be bad karma.

10. Raging Alcoholic Masquerading as a Wine Connoisseur

PROFILE

Ever since his wife left him for the carpenter, he's found solace in the nectar of the gods.

GIFT

A bottle of '73 Bordeaux that you can't open until you're divorced.

MOTTO

"Kids, life is all about wine, women, and song. Well, since the bitch left me, two out of three isn't bad."

FAME

Claims to be a personal friend of Francis Ford Coppola.

BENEFITS

Every year he takes the family on wine-tasting tours, from the Napa Valley to Burgundy, France.

DRAWBACKS

He gets to taste wine, you get grape Kool-Aid.

11. NASCAR Family

PROFILE

There's Ronnie, Mikey, Jenna, Ma, Pops, and Granddad Sal(vade). What a pissa. Sixty years off the boat and Sal still doesn't speak a word of English.

GIFT

The tickets to NASCAR fell through so you're getting an IOU again.

MOTTO

"Is it noon yet? Screw it, it's my house. It's always Miller Time."—Pops

FAME

Pops won $5,000 in a Lucky Duck scratch-off card and took the entire family out to the Olive Garden, before losing the rest on a bad tip at the track.

BENEFITS

No dress code.

DRAWBACKS

The kids practice their pro-wrestling moves on you.

12. The Child Substitute

PROFILE

He's treated way too well. He has the best pedigree in the family; gets a massage once a week at the Dog Spa; and if it wasn't for Carlee, the German shorthaired pointer, Pancake would have been Best in Show.

GIFT

A card from him with paw print signature.

MOTTO

"Be careful what you say around him; he understands everything."—Mr. Mitchell

WILL

He's in it, you're not.

BENEFITS

Always happy to see you and greet you with a sloppy kiss.

DRAWBACKS

Loves the crotch.

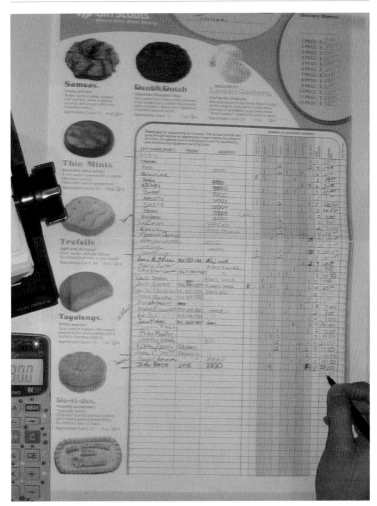

13. Girl Scout Troop Leader Mom

PROFILE

Every family member and office co-worker will be getting a call from this woman hawking cookies so her six-year-old can win an iPod mini.

GIFT

A copy of Dale Carnegie's *How to Win Friends and Influence People*—presented with absolutely no irony.

MOTTO

"Only three boxes! Come on, it's for a good cause. If you order five more, my Sierra meets her goal!"

SECRET

Sierra is defending her title as the best-selling scout two years running.

BENEFITS

Enough cookies to feed a village.

DRAWBACKS

Trans fats!

14. Gold Digger
(a.k.a. "Pumpkin")

PROFILE

Just like Anna Nicole Smith, she truly loves her much older, less attractive, extraordinarily wealthy husband.

GIFT

She gets, not gives.

MOTTO

"No money, no honey."

FAME

First on the block to get Botox injections.

BENEFITS

Having some eye candy at your family events isn't so bad.

DRAWBACKS

Can't help visualizing the sex.

REC 00:23:59

15. Uncle Stan the Camera Man

Thinks he's Ken Burns filming three-hour documentaries at every family event. Barbeques, reunions, funerals—is nothing sacred?

Every birthday he gives you a video he filmed at your birthday the previous year, peppered with witty commentary and homemade sound effects.

"Back up, you're ruining my shot. Okay, now do it again."

Determined to get on *America's Funniest Home Videos* with that clip of you getting hit in the crotch with a piñata bat.

He does a great Robin Leach.

Won't let you handle the camcorder. No way. Sorry, it's not a toy.

16. Slightly Racist Grandparent

PROFILE

Asians are Orientals, African Americans are blacks. You get the picture.

GIFT

You were hoping for the new Jay-Z CD. Instead you got Mel Torme on vinyl.

MOTTO

Unprintable.

SECRET

HUGE fan of Sammy Davis Jr.

BENEFITS

Most of her racist slurs are in Yiddish, so people don't understand them.

DRAWBACKS

If Archie Bunker had a sister, she'd be it.

17. Fanny, Not the Life of the Party

PROFILE

After escaping from the Cossacks in the middle of the night, she hid in the hold of a cargo ship leaving for America. She then settled on the Lower East Side of Manhattan, sold fruit, and resoled leather shoes.

GIFT

Fruit and shoes.

MOTTO

"Vut iz zis loud jazz, oy the meshuggener vith the horns!"

SECRET

Was a wild and crazy gal back in the '10s.

BENEFITS

Doesn't like to party, but sure could host one. In her cubby of a kitchen, she cooked Passover dinners for fifty.

DRAWBACKS

The kasha varniskas was always a bit dry.

18. Your Son, the Tenant

PROFILE

Had a job, then came the recession, got laid off. He now resides on your couch.

GIFT

A sixer of Busch.

MOTTO

"There are just no jobs right now for someone with my qualifications."

FAME

He's pitching a reality show to Fox called *Living La Vida Sofa.*

BENEFITS

You'll never have empty nest syndrome.

DRAWBACKS

He just started an online business—eBaying the heirlooms in the attic.

19. *America's Most Wanted* Cousin

He started out with petty stuff, stealing your Lincoln Logs, swiping a Matchbox car. But when he burned down your tree house, you decided it wasn't a good idea to share a bunk bed anymore.

An iPod with the serial number scratched off.

San Quentin, cellblock E.

He's been on national TV, twice. *Cops* counts.

Having a cousin in maximum-security prison gives you street cred.

If he breaks out, your house is the first stop.

20. Conversation Hijacker

She is ready to pounce like a cat into any conversation not involving her, and run with it as long as possible. Even though you've known her your entire life, Conversation Hijacker knows very little about you.

The five-speed hand blender she told you all about the last time you saw her.

"That reminds me of the time that I . . ."

Once met Gloria Estefan in waiting room of doctor's office, a story she'll bring up anytime you mention "song," "celebrity," "doctor," "office," "chair" or "salsa."

No need to watch *Entertainment Tonight.* She knows what's up.

Somehow it's a natural segue from Julia Roberts's life to hers.

21. Power-Hungry Hosts

PROFILE

They insist on monopolizing the family-function venue; their home is conveniently located at the epicenter of the core family.

GIFT

Because there are so many people at their home, their hospitality and graciousness are their gifts to you.

MOTTO

"Mi casa es su casa, but no eating in the living room."

SECRET

Barry can't drive. Got in a "slight" fender-bender and lost about ten points on his license, which has since been revoked. The wife has gephyrophobia, the fear of bridges.

BENEFITS

The wine floweth aplenty.

DRAWBACKS

They use place cards as strategically as the seating arrangement at the U.N.

22. Sister Who Was in *Girls Gone Wild*

PROFILE

Your older sister (third in her class) had a few Jägermeister shots at Señor Frog's in Cancún and decided to break out of her shell.

GIFT

Cash. It's more like hush money than a birthday gift.

MOTTO

"If you've got it, flaunt it."

SECRET

She was only pretending to be drunk.

BENEFITS

As a major dork, you've earned huge points among the cool kids.

DRAWBACKS

They ask for autographed copies.

23. Jewish Mother

PROFILE

The woman creates more drama than David E. Kelley. The worst vice is advice, and she has plenty, gems such as "What if you lose your job, what about that? You had to major in art history, didn't you. You can't even draw!"

GIFT

Costco, Wal-Mart, TJ Maxx, Filene's Basement—these are her hunting grounds for great bargains. Expect bulk.

MOTTO

"Why didn't you call? I called the police, the hospitals, and the morgue!"

HOME

Your room is exactly the way you left it, including the fake *Sports Illustrated* cover with your face, touting you as the 1985 NFL MVP.

BENEFITS

Would do anything for you.

DRAWBACKS

Constantly reminds you that she *has* done everything for you and what has she gotten in return? Nothing. You wouldn't even notice if she died. She went through eighteen hours of labor for this?

The Jenkins Family Gazette

MILTON JENKINS, EDITOR & PUBLISHER
Winter 2004

Uncle Carl Feeling Better!

Who knew that a rectal abscess could lay a person up for six weeks? Not me! But at long last, Uncle Carl has been given a clean bill of health from his proctologist, Alan Shapiro, at the Mount Sinai Medical Center.

Aunt Gladys is thrilled to have Uncle Carl up and around the house again. "I was sick of waiting on him hand and foot," she confided to me last week. "It's about time."

You can expect to see Aunt Gladys and Uncle Carl at Eli's Bar Mitzvah this coming May, where Uncle Carl

Uncle Carl

says he'll be. "Dancing the cha-cha with the best of them."

THIS JUST IN: The chest pain Uncle Carl experienced last week was just gas.

Mr. Snickets Still Missing

Grandma Rose's orange tabby Mr. Snickets is still missing after being accidentally let out of the house by a repairman who was fixing the refrigerator last Thursday.

Her other three cats, Carmela, Bentley McGee, and Hollis Menudo are quite distraught and haven't been eating, she reported to me on Monday.

Sources say that the Kelly kid who lives down the street could have had a hand in Mr. Snickets' disappearance, but reports are inconclusive.

"Mr. Snickets is a fairly adept mouse catcher, so I don't think that he'll starve," Grandma Rose said. "But it has been pretty cold lately, and Mr. Snickets isn't a big fan of

Mr. Tabbyfoot Snickets

the snow. He also hates the rain."

If you've seen Mr. Snickets, or have any information on his whereabouts, please contact Grandma Rose immediately.

THIS JUST IN: Mr. Snickets was spotted near the dumpster outside the Olive Garden on Elm Street. The search continues!

24. Family Newsletter Publisher

PROFILE

Founder, publisher, editor, reporter, and head of ad sales for monthly family newsletter.

GIFT

Complimentary Jenkins Family Wall Calender: $9.95 retail value. You might even get your name in the Who's Who or BIG Announcement section.

MOTTO

"Is this off the record?"

FAME

Was the first to break the story of Cousin Henry's hip replacement.

BENEFITS

Now that he's gone online, he sends the newsletter via e-mail. And because he works on an IBM clone with outdated PrintShop software, no one can open the attachment.

DRAWBACKS

He sells his address list to credit card companies.

25. Wife Who Put Your Son in Ballet

Billy Elliot spawned a new generation of boy ballet dancers in Britain and America. However, *Friday Night Lights* is more your kind of movie.

You gave him a subscription to *Sports Illustrated* and every piece of sports equipment a boy could ever want, and snuck him some old *Playboys* from the closet. Your wife got him the leotard he always wanted.

"Watch this Dad, a plié!"

She installed a leaning bar in the playroom.

Ballet dancers build great leg strength and can become accomplished football kickers. They also get all the ballerinas, which makes every dad proud.

Your son wears tights.

		From	Subject
✉ 📎		Al Greenberg	Fw: Hotel Burj al Arab
✉		Al Greenberg	Fw: irish?
✉		Al Greenberg	Fw: God's new Policy
✉ 📎		Al Greenberg	Fw: [Fwd: Fw: Inner Strength]
✉ 📎		Al Greenberg	Fw: FW: Enjoy web link
✉ 📎		Al Greenberg	Fw: Check out MasterOni This is great!
✉		Al Greenberg	Fw: ADULT FAIRY TALES
✉		Al Greenberg	Spam: Fw: Little Pedro
✉		Al Greenberg	Fw: THE RULES OF FLYING (priceless!)
✉		Al Greenberg	Fw: Grandparents! Listen Closely!
✉		Al Greenberg	Fw: Have you seen this man?
✉		Al Greenberg	Fw: check this out
✉		Al Greenberg	Born To Brothels
✉		Al Greenberg	Fw: America's Has-Been Economy
✉		Al Greenberg	Fw: News & Views 03.10.05
✉		Al Greenberg	Fw: Funny
✉		Al Greenberg	Fw:
✉		Al Greenberg	Fw: THE VALUE OF ANGER
✉		Al Greenberg	Fw: No Subject
✉ 📎		Al Greenberg	Emailing: 0223-08
✉		Al Greenberg	Spam: Fw: MEN STRIKE BACK
✉		Al Greenberg	Fw: Tell Congress to repair our election sys...
✉		Al Greenberg	Fw: fwd - marriage ceremony
✉		Al Greenberg	Fw: fwd - chinese wedding night
✉ 📎		Al Greenberg	Fw: Confidence In The Status Of Future S...

26. Family E-mail Forwarder

PROFILE

With the push of a button every family member's inbox is overflowing with photos, jokes, inspirational stories, and virus warnings—four times a day.

GIFT

A 3MB e-mail containing a picture of a crying baby in front of a birthday cake with the caption "It's somebody's Berfffday!"

MOTTO

"This is really funny! Had to forward it along!"

HOME

He lives alone and has way too much time on his hands.

BENEFITS

Your spam filter catches most of his e-mails.
(Heaven forbid he gets your IM.)

DRAWBACKS

He forwards you every one of those e-mails that say Bill Gates will pay them ten dollars for each person to whom you forward that e-mail.

27. Glory Days Dad

PROFILE

He was in a 1965 issue of *Sports Illustrated* in "College Football Players to Watch" but blew out his knee in the home opener. Has since shoved sports down his children's throats.

GIFT

Some sort of ball.

MOTTO

"You call that a spiral? Come on! Bring your A game."

WARDROBE

Nine to five he's in a suit. Before, after, and on the weekends, it's sweats, headband, whistle, clipboard, and athletic supporter.

BENEFITS

Last year he threatened your JV coach's life and since then you get lots of playing time.

DRAWBACKS

If you're his wife, kiss your backyard goodbye. He blacktopped over it to make a full basketball court.

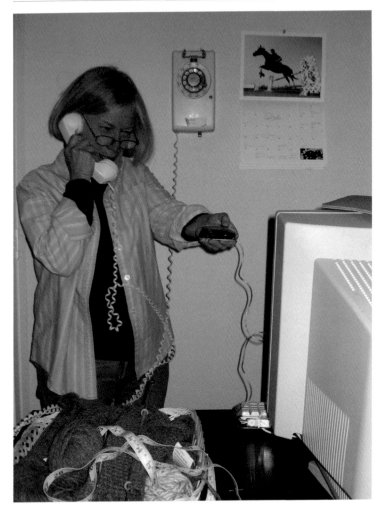

28. The Computer-Illiterate Generation

PROFILE

In an effort to stay current, they finally bought a PC. Now they call you up like a twenty-four-hour technical support hotline.

GIFT

Since figuring out eBay, they have been buying you snow globes from every major European city. The one from Prague is actually kind of cool.

MOTTO

"The screen froze. I think I did something. Can you come over?"

SECRET

Internet porn.

BENEFITS

In two years they'll have completed the family tree using genealogy software. That's one less show-and-tell project you'll have to help your kids with.

DRAWBACKS

Now that you're a "computer genius," you're fielding calls from Grandpa Dave and Aunt Ruthie's neighbor, Betty.

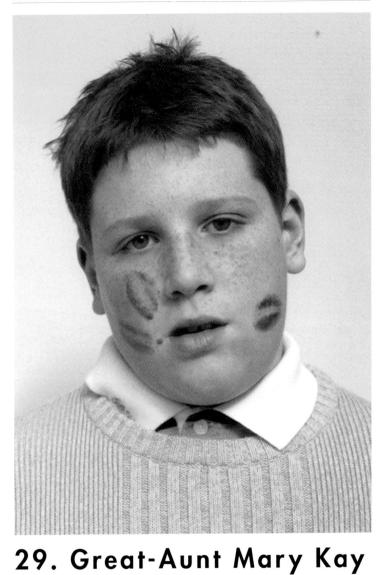

29. Great-Aunt Mary Kay

Your mother's aunt is more a billboard for a cosmetics counter than anything else.

Once a Mary Kay saleswoman, she unloads extra inventory stored in her garage on birthdays and at Christmas.

"Even if you're a boy, a little foundation and rouge never hurts."

Wears maraschino cherry lipstick, the same color Loni Anderson did on *WKRP in Cincinnati.*

You can't lie: she's got some full, supple lips.

You've noticed that since her eyesight has waned, she's beginning to come dangerously close to your mouth when she kisses you hello.

30. Brother Who Beat the Crap out of You

PROFILE

Your older brother reminds you that you are an uninvited guest in his world—a world of pain that rains down atomic wedgies, noogies, and purple nurples.

GIFT

One punch per year. An extra hard one for good luck.

MOTTO

"Want to go on a little trip?"
—Said right before he zipped you up in a suitcase and punted it down the steps

SECRET

He wets his bed.

BENEFITS

Indian burns are his way of saying *I love you*.

DRAWBACKS

Your elementary school teacher called in Social Services when she noticed black-and-blue marks all over your arms.

31. Power Couple

PROFILE

They live in a museum. Look but don't touch. Stand but do *not* sit—especially at the Queen Anne table.

GIFT

$100 check that somehow they manage to write off.

MOTTO

"You can admire it *from a distance*."

HOME

It's the one behind the Beamer and the Range Rover.

BENEFITS

If you're nice, you might get a Kandinsky when they kick.

DRAWBACKS

They read *Architectural Digest* like a mail-order catalog, saying "have it, have it, need it, have it." You just read *TV Guide*.

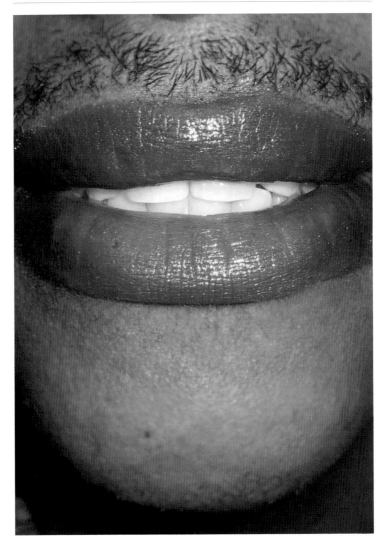

32. Maunt

PROFILE

Half man, half aunt, she was handed down an extra male chromosome, sideburns, and a slight 'stache.

GIFT

Ironically, she got you your first shaving set at age thirteen.

MOTTO

"Come and give your aunt Bernice a kiss."

SECRET

Rumor has it among the younger cousins that Maunt was the bearded lady in the county fair.

BENEFITS

As a child you prayed Maunt did not pass down her genes to you. Later you found out she's not blood.

DRAWBACKS

From early on you develop NFL running-back type moves to avoid rubbing cheeks with her hairy mole.

33. The Early Leavers

PROFILE

They can't stay because they have more important things to do.

GIFT

No time for that. Time is money.

MOTTO

"Sorry, we can't stay long because _____
                                        (Early Leaver)
has a _____ at the _____that,
         (name of function)   (hotel)
sadly, we must attend. Kiss kiss."

FAME

The cameo appearance gives them a superhero mystique, as if they are always running off on some secret mission.

BENEFITS

Not around long enough to eat too much.

DRAWBACKS

Not around long enough to feel obligated to bring you something.

34. Slutty First Cousin

PROFILE

Sister of the guido Brothers Gamboni, she's the one wearing hot pants to Christmas dinner and who brings her thirty-four-year-old boyfriend, lead singer of a Guns N' Roses tribute band.

GIFT

She found out you were a virgin, so she set you up with her girlfriend Gina.

MOTTO

"Tantric is overrated."

FAME

She was on *The Real World*. Not as a cast member but one of the girls who slept with a guy on the show.

BENEFITS

Her hair, big. Her boobs, bigger.

DRAWBACKS

Dated the entire basketball team, including Coach Bossone. But you still got cut from JV.

35. Religious Zealots

PROFILE

This side of the family just found Jesus. Actually, they found him in a Big Mac at McDonald's, his likeness appearing in ketchup smeared on the bun.

GIFT

A Gideon Bible with their favorite psalms highlighted, with a handy carrying case so you can read it on the bus.

MOTTO

"God hates the sin but loves the sinner. Have faith and I'm sure you won't get much jail time for the DUI."

FAME

Have the only year-round manger scene in the neighborhood.

BENEFITS

They make a mean Jesus cake.

DRAWBACKS

Are convinced you're going to burn in eternal hellfire if you do not take Jesus Christ as your savior immediately —a fact that they bring up at every family occasion.

36. The Force Feeder

PROFILE

She has transferred her fear of losing money to fear of losing pounds. Visit her house and you're not going home until your cholesterol is 240.

GIFT

A savings bond for fifty dollars, so when it matures you can take yourself to Sizzler.

MOTTO

"Eat, eat. You're skin and bones!"

FAME

At Thanksgiving, she has an annual Weigh-In. Relatives weigh themselves when they walk in the door and when they leave. Greatest gain gets a prize.

BENEFITS

Chopped liver and brisket taste good.

DRAWBACKS

Borscht does not.

37. Cheek Pincher

PROFILE

Not to be outdone by Firm Handshaker (no. 4), Cheek Pincher has a fierce grip and is blessed with nieces with chubby cheeks.

GIFT

Paid for your braces, which dig into your cheeks when she pinches you.

MOTTO

"Is that a gorgeous face? Is that not just delicious?"

SECRET

She, too, was pinched as a child.

BENEFITS

Now that Cheek Pincher uses a walker, she can't sneak up on you as quickly as she used to.

DRAWBACKS

If she gets a good lock on you, she'll break a capillary.

38. Résumé-Padding Parents

PROFILE

Colleges like extracurricular activities, and extracurricular activities they shall have. In addition to playing the tuba, their kids are on the chess team, are national spelling bee runners-up, and read to blind children on the weekends.

GIFT

A dog-eared copy of *Learn to Speed Read in 21 Days*.

MOTTO

"Honey, you sound lovely. Just two more hours."

SECRET

The kids need to get scholarships because the parents invested heavily in dot-coms.

BENEFITS

The plan worked. She got into Dartmouth.

DRAWBACKS

The plan failed. At Dartmouth, she smokes more pot than Cheech and Chong combined and fails out first semester.

39. Monopoly Bank Thief

PROFILE

Her five-year unbeaten streak in Monopoly, Clue, the Game of Life, and Candyland came into question when you caught her with a wad of hundreds stuffed in her sock.

GIFT

Unexpectedly, something nice. (She's flush after robbing your piggy bank.)

MOTTO

"Finders keepers, losers weepers."

FAME

Last year she set up a tiny videocamera pointed at the Christmas tree to prove to her first-grade class that Santa does not exist.

BENEFITS

If she's feeling generous, she'll give you a free pass when you land on St. Charles Place.

DRAWBACKS

Stealing funny money is a gateway to more serious crimes such as dealing Uno cards from the bottom of the deck.

40. The Holiday Drunk

The life of the party until he gets so wasted that he goes outside and shovels snow in the dark, yelling "Rage, rage against the dying of the light!"

Got you a flask for your eighteenth.

During a bender he stuffed a tape recorder inside the turkey to see what his wife and in-laws said about him when he went off to shovel snow.

Falls asleep in the bathroom every year. You have to get out the screwdriver and take off the hinges.

Hysterical for the first two hours when he's a "happy drunk." He slurs great Sinatra standards like "My Way" and "One for My Baby."

Not so fun when "happy drunk" moves into "emotional-angry-drunk," dredging up everything bad done to him when he was a child. Like the time his father was playing knee-pony and replaced him with another child. "It ruined me!"

41. The Martha Wannabe

PROFILE

Notice the squash bird centerpiece. The woman spent one hour on the carrot feet alone.

GIFT

Something that obviously reflected a lot of thought, effort, and time.

MOTTO

"Move over. *I'll* carve the turkey."

HOME

Don't even get me started.

BENEFITS

The woman can cook.

DRAWBACKS

For her son's second birthday she made Elmo cupcakes, Cookie Monster cookies, *and* a tiered SpongeBob SquarePants layer cake. For your child's birthday you bought an Entenmann's raspberry danish.

42. Shrimp Ring Bringer

Profoundly deluded, Shrimp Ring Bringer envisions this plentiful and economical shrimp platter, with cocktail sauce, as the centerpiece around which the whole family will gather.

GIFT

Anything on sale. A frog or butterfly brooch found at a TJ Maxx close-out.

MOTTO

"The food wasn't very good, but what big portions!"

SECRET

Allergic to shellfish.

BENEFITS

It's better than bringing nothing.

DRAWBACKS

Actually, it would be better if she brought nothing. $5.99 for thirty shrimp? You can't get a five-piece shrimp cocktail for six dollars. Be afraid. Be very afraid.

43. The Vegan

PROFILE

The Vegan is a pariah, insisting on "humane" food alternatives to the traditional carnivorous Thanksgiving Day meal.

GIFT

24-pack of organic, dairy-free, gluten-free, no-carb snack bars.

MOTTO

"This holiday is more about the flavors of the harvest than butchering live animals. Sadly, it has been altered to fit America's insatiable appetite for flesh." But if that's true, did they eat soybean pie at the first Thanksgiving?

SECRET

She loves McDonald's.

BENEFITS

Every year Uncle Frank slips some dark meat in the Tofurky and waits for her to scream.

DRAWBACKS

Vegans are just weird.

44. David Copperfieldstein

Master illusionist Uncle Dave has performed the same magic tricks every year since you were five.

The Magic Trick Chest, Jr. Contents include the amazing bending magic wand, the everlasting handkerchief, and the floating dollar (dollar not included).

"Hey, what's that behind your ear?"

Fooled Grandma Jenkins three times in a row. (It should be noted, she has glaucoma.)

After he does the trick, he lets you keep the magic quarter.

Makes you shout the magic word, "Scrumpledoggins," to get the quarter.

45. Inappropriate Uncle

PROFILE

Entertains with such parlor tricks as burping the alphabet backward.

GIFT

A gift certificate for two to Hooters.

MOTTO

"If there's anything I've learned in life it's to never let them see you sweat. Or naked after a swim in the ocean."

FAME

Sends crude e-mails to you at work of fat ladies sunbathing nude.

BENEFITS

He's a laugh riot at times and has the biggest heart you know. If you needed it, he'd give you his liver. Unfortunately he could use a new one himself.

DRAWBACKS

Has five sexual harassment cases pending against him. All by relatives.

Terry Jamison
Linda Jamison

46. Psychic Twins

PROFILE

Terry and Linda got the "gift." At holiday functions, they are mobbed by the relatives who want to know if so-and-so is cheating on them or if Google's stock price has peaked.

GIFT

A free half-hour session ($150 value!)

MOTTO

"Come and play with us, Danny. Forever and ever and ever."

SECRET

They only predicted seven Golden Globe winners in 2005.

BENEFITS

You put money down on five of those seven.

DRAWBACKS

They foresaw the outcome of your marriage on your first date, but didn't tell you.

47. Condescending Shirley

She was once married but it ended unpleasantly. Ever since, she has become a Joan Rivers without the microphone, hosting from the couch.

"She actually thinks she can pull off that dress."

"My schnauzer wouldn't touch this cordon bleu. I'll get something later at Taco Bell."

"It's so sad. Everyone knew he was sleeping with the intern but her. It's so sad."

"The lawsuit hasn't gone through, but my lawyer says he'll be lucky if gets to keep his bus pass."

"She's definitely on the cocktail: Prozac and chardonnay with a splash of Valium."

48. Kissing Cousins

PROFILE

Grandma Norma set these two up at Christmas last year. Who knew Uncle Mort's daughter would be such a looker?

GIFT

She gave him a framed photograph of them bathing together as children.

MOTTO

"What's the big deal? It's legal to marry cousins in twenty-six states, just not ours."

SECRET

Albert Einstein's parents were cousins.
FDR and Eleanor Roosevelt were cousins.
Rudolph Giuliani was briefly married to a second cousin. Heck, everyone's doing it these days.

BENEFITS

Everything stays in the family.

DRAWBACKS

. . . especially the DNA.

49. Bald Side of the Family

PROFILE

Abraham begat Isaac, who begat Jacob, who down the line begat Grandpa, who begat your father, who begat you . . . a cue ball chrome dome.

GIFT

You were hoping for a prescription for Extra-strength Rogaine. You got a 20-speed Trek and a Livestrong bracelet instead.

MOTTO

"What we Rosenbergs lack up here, we make up for down there."

SECRET

Grandpa is only one quarter Jewish. The yarmulke is just a cover.

BENEFITS

They say the bald gene comes from the mother's side of the family.

DRAWBACKS

Your mother's stash of Halloween wigs is unusually extensive . . .

50. Mother-in-Law

PROFILE

You were not her first-round draft pick. As her daughter-in-law, you have discovered she does not understand the word "boundary" but knows plenty about the Oedipus complex.

GIFT

For your husband's birthday, she likes to take him out to his favorite restaurant and give him a few hundred-dollar bills, saying "Buy something for *yourself*, for a change."

MOTTO

When you were engaged and staying over at her house you heard her on the telephone with her friend: "Gloria, it's not over until he's walking down the aisle."

FAME

She didn't speak to you for a year after you mistakenly forwarded her a list of mother-in-law jokes, such as
Q: How do you stop your MIL from drowning?
A: Take your foot off her head.

BENEFITS

She likes to dredge up "priceless" dated, moth-balled items like her mink coat and "generously" hand them down to you. Immediately donate them to Goodwill and take the tax write-off.

DRAWBACKS

Bad move. She'll ask to borrow it for your son's christening.

51. Your Relative

PROFILE

GIFT

MOTTO

FAME

BENEFITS

DRAWBACKS

PORTRAIT PHOTOGRAPHY BY JULIE SOEFER
Makeup Artist: Beth Taranto
Photo remastering: Jason Meehan
Some old photos courtesy of Dead Fred Genealogy Photo Archive
   (www.deadfred.com)
SNAPATORIUM Original Vintage Photographs

ADDITIONAL PHOTOGRAPHERS:
Perfect Family: CORBIS
Child Substitute: Brian Mitchell
Conversation Hijacker: Greg Lowery (illustrator)
Brother Who Beat the Crap out of You: Ellen K. Racz
Sister Who Was in *Girls Gone Wild*: Cheyenne De Rosario
Other Girls Who Went Wild: Jayson Atienza
Force Feeder: Mrs. Schwartz
Wife Who Put Your Son in Ballet: Mrs. Bethany
Power-Hungry Hosts: Lori Smyth
Power Couple: Zoe Heighington
Psychic Twins: Caine/Digitrope.com
Jewish Mother: Melissa Liebling-Goldberg
Résumé-Padding Parents: Cindy Soefer

THE PHOTOGRAPHED:
Great-Aunt Mary Kay: Aaron Lang
Kissing Cousins: Jessie Resnick and Alli Alemi
Jewish Mother: Brenda Liebling Goldberg
Monopoly Bank Thief: Rachel and Jackie Resnik
Inga: Robert, Sheri, Robert Jr., Jackie Fleishman; and Inga
Ballet Dancer: Hunter Bethany
Child Substitute: Pancake
America's Most Wanted Cousin (reenactor): Ethan Baum
Inappropriate Uncle: Uncle Louie, Cassandra Palacio
Slightly Racist Grandparent: Sue Berger
Slutty Cousin: Cheyanne de Rosario
Raging Alcoholic: Dan Leeds
Holistic New Age Aunt: Basia
Carl: William N. Collins
Michael Pessi: Himself
Gold-Digger (a.k.a Pumpkin): Christiana Amorosia
Glory Days Dad: Bruce Maltz
Power Couple: Annie and Jimmy Angellino

Thank You All:

Dunow, Carlson & Lerner
Colin Dickerman
Marisa Pagano
Alona Fryman
Suzie Lee
Yelena Gitlin
Panio Gianopoulos
Andrew Ritter
Jeannette Balleza
Kate Mahar
Alex Finkelstein
Jay Tandon
The D'Agostinos
Alan Paul
Scott Mitnick
Greg Racz
Ellen Racz
Annie Cooper
Tanya Choi
Matt Richards
Andy Finnel
Enzo Velazquez
Denise Weber
Lauren Cofield
Bonnie Levine
Chris Barnett
Jamie Tanaka
Jason Meehan
Josh Cahill
Grandpa
Grandma
Mary's at Baldwin Creek
Linda, Doug and
   daughter
Dr. Soefer
Cindy Soefer
Stacy Soefer
Michele Soefer
Mark Schmulen
Helen Greene
Debra Falcone
Hollie Bethany
Lou Irizarry
Katie Rosin, immensely

Omri Green
Carola
Carola's boyfriend, Rob
Their dog, Amelia
Chad Urmston
Guys from character
   camp
Meira Cohen
Melinda Ward
Jayson Atienza
Frank Anselmo
Kelli Milne
Mary Tucker
Liz Abate
Greg Mascolo
Glenn Brown
Sherrod Melvin
Thomas
Ian Brand
Jackie Enfield
Maria Pappalardo
Danny Roth
Sue Berger
Judy Wolf
Janelle Barnao
Kit Campbell
Stuart Johnson
Rachel Gradstein
Seth Lieberman
Ashley Blake Fisher
Cheryl Dunn
Matthew Dunn
Courtney Dunn
Aaron Dunn
William N. Collins
Sharon Collins
Mario Giacalone
Elisa Resnik
Yan Xi
Christiana Amorosia
Kelly Rophele
Rob Seitelman
Lesley Miller
Samantha Roberts

Shannon Duletzke
Lori Segal
Lesley Freedman
Kim and Chuck
Daniel Racz
Alexa Jervis
Laurel Tyndale
Kyle Jenkins
Janelle Barnao
Elise Daher
Brandi Jenna
Tami Lacertos
The Mahars
Nate Taylor
Victoria Lesiw
Erik Bjordklund
Amy Cook
Philip Thomas
Harriet Gordon and Kids
Will Steacy
Stephen C. Solosky
Lauren Dub
Jackie Resnik
Barbara Sullivan
Beth Safrank
Sharon Jessen
Josh Neuman
Wendy Morris
Kew
William N. Collins
Mario Giacalone
Chuck
Rob Seitleman
Deborah Lester
Melissa
   Liebling-Goldberg
Michael Perri
Eric Van Skyhawk
Martha Gay
Ivan Cohen
Debora Falcone
Mat Bisher
and everyone else that
   I forgot. Sorry.

A Note on the Author

Justin Racz is an advertising copywriter.
He is the author of *J.Crewd* and *50 Jobs Worse Than Yours*.
He lives in New York City.